Desire Lines

Stephen Boyce

To the Lucky Winner
Thank you Anne.

Stephen

arrowhead
poetry

First published 2010 by
Arrowhead Press
70 Clifton Road, Darlington
Co. Durham, DL1 5DX
Tel: (01325) 260741

Typeset in 11 on 14pt Laurentian by
Arrowhead Press

Email: editor@arrowheadpress.co.uk
Website: http://www.arrowheadpress.co.uk

ISBN 978-1-904852-27-8

Printed in Great Britain by the MPG Books Group, Bodmin and King's Lynn

for Sioban

Acknowledgements

Thanks are due to the editors of the following publications in which some of these poems first appeared: *The Interpreter's House, Acumen, Smiths Knoll, the Southern Daily Echo, The Stanza, Poems 22* (Lancaster Litfest), and the 2002 and 2003 Ware Poets competition anthologies.

'The Seventh Wave' won first prize in the 1999 Kent & Sussex Poetry Competition; 'Knokke-le-Zoute' won first prize in the Leicester Open Poetry Competition 2000, and 'Chaos Theory' was awarded third prize in the 2001 Ledbury Festival competition.

My warm thanks to Simon Richey and Keiren Phelan for constant support and encouragement.

Jacket Illustration:

"…beaten-down paths in the grass, known as 'desire lines' in planning-speak, indicate yearning."

John LaPlante, chief traffic engineer for TY International

"Desire lines (or natural desire lines, as they're also called)…are never perfectly straight. Instead, like a river, they meander this way and that, as if to prove that desire itself isn't linear and (literally, in this case) straightforward."
Paul McFedries

Contents

One

Two

Three

Four

One

Chaos Theory

Even this soft farewell has the air
of an echo, its frayed edge brushing
the ear as if from afar;
it falls with a yellow maple leaf
in the Parc Bordelais, settles
on gravel beneath green metal chairs;
it is the sound my fingers make
tracing the line of your shin-bone
in the darkness; it is enough
to alert the police to seal off the town,
thinking there are men on the roof.
I will hear it again whenever
that flitting wren darts for cover
or just before her song shimmers the air.

Hold Still

In the hallway the brass corners
and polished surface of the military chest
reflect our faces. The drawer purrs
and clicks as he opens it, lets the flap drop.
A smell of camphor. He takes out
an oblong wooden box, removes
the tissue paper, weighs four silver medals
in his palm, smoothes the ribbons of red,
green, blue and gold. He holds them
against his brushed black overcoat.
In the mirror he pins them – quite straight –
across his neat lapel. He smiles,
looks down at me. "Hold still," he says,
fixing the poppy in my buttonhole.

Photographing Marjorie

He has contrived it so that everything
is at a jaunty angle; the brim
of your summer hat, your smile, the ship's slim
rail which you are leaning back on
in your white raincoat – collar halfway
up – the matching clutch bag, even the spray
from the tipsy waves. He is pleased with the line
of your gaze – past his shoulder, towards Dieppe
perhaps – so that I can almost see him step
back, the silver Voigtlander pressed to his cheek,
adjusting the focus ring as he squints
through the viewfinder. The light glints
on the sea. He holds you both in this moment
for ever, one seen, the other not, like the weave
of sun and shadow in the folds of your sleeve.

In the Darkroom

In the red glow of the darkroom
my father taught me how to process film.
His hand on mine, we slid
the paper through the liquid,
a dry smell lingering
on yellowing fingertips.
Tipping the dish, we watched
little waves ripple over
the smooth emulsion
and we waited.

Slowly, seeping through pale sheen
as if emerging from heat haze,
came the faintest grey image,
clearer, sharper, closer
as the seconds ticked away
until, peering through the gloom,
I saw in perfect contrast
the picture I had framed,
until I saw my father's face,
lustrous in the tray.

Now, as if failing to fix that image,
he has begun to fade away.
Little by little his face is
wreathed again in mist,
slips back inside the paper,
features diminishing, shadow
bleached out and vanishing,
so that all that is left to me
when I turn on the light
is this clean white sheet.

Knokke le Zoute

You could hire a kind of go-kart, a squat
four-wheeled pedal bike, and swerve at speed
along the promenade unnerving grannies
or some yapping pooch. Or you could pitch
and roll across the dunes and – furtively –
among the marram grass, observe
the glistening sungirls oil their burnished skin –
disturbing for a twelve-year-old. And when
they headed for the bar or flirted
at the water's edge, you could pour the hot
and honeyed lotion through sandy fingers,
fill up their high-heeled shoes, breathe the dangerous
smell of perfumed leather, swerving
into the clammy mysteries of sex.

Skin
i.m. EMB

Her skin seems to have absorbed
all the millions of minute
particles of talcum applied day by day,
so that her cheek resembles
the powder puff itself
and the slightest touch
might float a tiny perfumed cloud
from the soft folds of her face.

When the kettle spills
her skin soaks up the scalding water
like a worn sponge.

Lighthouse
i.m. GWB

His pencil shuffles across the page
in one unbroken tangled line
like the strings of ginger tobacco
his trembling fingers tease
into the little machine
in which he rolls his cigarettes.
A tiny landscape appears,
a lighthouse takes shape on a headland,
seabirds scour the cliffs
above breaking surf.

He smiles a smoke-stained smile
and the paper flutters towards me
in his outstretched hand.

An Outdoor Life

When Great Uncle Frank came over from Vancouver
he brought the Great Outdoors.

It blew through the hallway at Regent Road
trembling the steady pendulum

of the grandfather clock, rousing its moon-
and-stars face; in the front parlour

it skittered into beads that fringed the domed
silk lampshade, stirred the chenille cloth

on which Grandma taught me
beggar-my-neighbour and patience.

In his check shirt, braces and moleskins
he was pylons and railroad tracks,

the smell of timber, the glow of the firebox;
his head a soft white cloud

billowing, and when he spoke
the Pacific sighed through huge sequoias.

He made straight for the garden, neat as it was.

Re-planting

Lifting the cyclamen,
its clod of earth comfortable in my fingers,
I feel I am lifting your bones.

You left me with a dead weight,
but these corms and springy ringlets
are heart-light in my palm.

Pink shells perched on their stems
vibrate to the soft cooing
of doves in the chimney

and I hear you clearing
your throat again
as you turn the page.

A mix of clag and grit
clings to the grain of my fingers,
so often held in yours.

A robin approaches
flicking earth into the tiny grave
I've cleared of ivy and worms.

Two

For Better or Worse

She is running down the alley,
running for her life, in her grasp
a suitcase filled with knives and forks
that rattles like a cashbox
with the rhythm of her stride.

In her mind she hears the slap
of wash between the boat hulls –
water again, it's all water
this bond, this fluid connection
between mother and daughter.

Even running away there's something
she's running towards, for better or worse.

It begins to rain, falls like needles,
touchneedles of copper and gold
that strike the cobbled dock beneath her
bobby-socked and sandled feet,
sparking, lighting the quay on which
he stands, tall and uniformed.

She stops. She knows he's hers.

His Voice

She loves the sound of his voice;
it reminds her of walnuts
and apricots, the red soil
of the orchard.
                    When he sings
to her she sees white geese
slipstream each other
wedge-shaped over the delta,
reed beds dancing in a warm half-light;
she hears echoes of the sea,
the familiar stirring of shingle
like atoms of memory
in motion.

His words are singular as
the thumbprint's soft vortex.

After Benjamin Franklin

Your affectionate touch
like my knuckle to the key
drew lightning from heaven,
left a scorch mark on my flesh
and an indelible scent.

I am learning to live with it.

Beyond Forensics

According to Lockhart's principle
when two objects meet, touch,
they exchange something of each other.

We met and microscopic spores
crossed continents, travelled through time zones.
Like camel trains on the great Silk Road

my fingertips traced ribbons of trade
this way and that across the ridge
of your shoulder, through the sleek hairs

of your neck leaving spices and oils,
collecting in return fine silk thread
exotic perfumes that lingered in the night.

But there is something beyond forensics,
something Lockhart didn't reckon with:
traces not revealed, such as the glances

we exchanged, almost imperceptible,
that static charge, a quickening in the air,
the touch of words – borrowed or bestowed –

and especially the silences between them:
bare leaves beneath snow-covered branches,
shadows that disappear with the thaw.

Once

Just say my name for me.
Say my name, once.

Call my name softly
across the valley;
I will hear you.
Remind me what is possible;
your voice like the wings
of this damsel fly
hovering in autumn sun.

Just say my name;
hearing you will complete me,
seeing you will ennoble me.

Just look my way
from the hillside where you stand.
One glance
I will see you.
Remind me what is possible;
your heliograph eyes
pinpointing this spider
that floats from my sleeve
on invisible thread.

Just look my way.
Say my name, once.

The Man

He wanted to be the man
who was wholly the man
he wanted to be.

The man whose presence
arose from the soles of his feet,
seeped through his ligaments
inhabiting a space
precisely the shape
he wanted to be.

He wanted to move freely
among crowds
with the freedom he felt
in fields or open water
where an aura,
a kind of evaporation of spirit,
announced the man
he wanted to be:

a man whose head
shed light on his shoulders
and hers when she bent
to kiss him – and also
the space between them
whenever they were apart.

He wanted to trust himself
the way the wind does
or the tide coming in;
he wanted to hold the centre
unembellished, raw
and free of pain;
he wanted to venture
and not betray himself.

He wanted to be the man
who was wholly the man
he wanted to be.

Entertaining Strangers

An angel came to him in his room
having heard he was dying.
She entered silently but the light
fell across his eyes like a blade.

There was nothing he could do.
She saw the livid skin and the patched head,
its rough sutures like scorched whiskers
on a pork roast, and the blood that matted his hair.

He knew from her silence they would not meet again,
she was shocked by his one-room world,
the grey walls, the smell from his drains
and the noise of the traffic below.

He let her go (and the angels sighed "Not again"),
she had seen herself nursing him,
wiping his brow with her pale hand
but this, this was no place to entertain strangers.

The Seventh Wave

He craned out over the edge as,
seventy feet below, seventy-five feet
four inches from his eye level,
hard against the foot of the cliff,
a strip of pale sand slid into view
like a letter slipped under the door.

Pulling back he remembered pebbles,
shells of all sorts, cork, rope,
fisherman's net and other flotsam,
seaweed of different colours,
driftwood in amusing shapes,
debris and detritus from other shores.

At low tide he had walked out
a quarter of a mile and had to wave
so that they knew he was still their loved one,
lured by the fascination of the sea,
the uncertainty of the distant horizon
and maybe one far, red sail.

At high tide he had been engulfed,
the seventh wave exploded round
his shoulders pounding the shore
to the pulse of the deep ocean,
drowning all his senses
laying him flat, drenched to the skin.

He had given up then, embraced
solitude, fixed his eye on the rocks,
anchored himself to the surface of things
while the sun burned a mirror
of his loneliness in the white sand
seventy feet below, or more.

The Lopsided Heart
for Jo

If he listens carefully in the dark
he can tell by the sound
which item of clothing she is removing:
the whisper of a silk slip,
the faint breath of nylons,
a soft click as she unhooks her bra.

In the early morning garden
he is close enough
to hear the air pass her lips,
to catch her familiar scent
even among the perfumes
of her roses and favourite honeysuckle.

On Valentine's Day he places
a token in her path, a shale heart,
lopsided like the real thing,
and as true as the words
on his headstone. She stoops
and with her fingers she can hear him sing.

Homecoming

Wait for me in the arrival lounge,
carry your pink umbrella,
wear pink gloves and the tea-plate hat
with its swaying feather.
Bring flowers if you wish –
something delicate with Gypsophila.

Dr and Mrs Kretchmar are going on
to Oxford, Le Manoir aux Quat' Saisons.
Mr Iskandarani is also
being met – he need not detain us,
likewise the Unaccompanied Minors
flying home to Oslo.

There are creases in my linen suit
and my hair is all over the place
but I'm longing to see you
– it's your stillness I'll notice first.
I hope I don't smudge your careful make-up.
I am trying to recall your face.

Three

Beached

We half undressed
in the orange glow of your gas fire
each caress releasing a shiver.

It's all there as if beached in
white sand; the soft touch
of your cheek, the curve

of your breast, the slope
of your pale hips, warm silences,
lips brushing thighs,

the unfathomable sweep
of your spine, and always
your ocean eyes.

Lens

*"What looks large from a distance, close up
ain't never that big".* Bob Dylan

From here it looks as though she's smiling
through those long feathered lashes.
It's all in the eyes.

It seems she wants to tell me something,
wants me to remember how the sun
burned into the hill

irradiating us with its great glass eye,
and how next morning I found
its cool reflection

in that tiny concave lens, still slick,
spit-coated, floating on beads of dew,
a miniature coracle

with the curve of her smile.

Where the Wind Stops

I am most myself among lichens and mosses,
Devon sandstone, hart's tongue and red campion,
oak leaves, hazel rods, chestnuts in their prickly pods.

For you can tell where the footpath floods in winter
by the abundance of ferns, wild garlic and smoothed stones.
You can tell by the way the grass bends, where the fox

and the badger run; by the curve and slant
of treetops, or the sudden swerve of a bird in flight,
which way the wind blows and where it stops.

Also Known as Fireweed

Was it Wast Water? Ennerdale?
Perhaps I dreamt it. All I remember
is hart's tongue, some red campion
and rosebay willowherb, its pink spires
crowding the lane on both sides,
the blooms going to seed from the bottom up,
and you peeling back the willing curlicue
of fruit to release flights of white down
into a cloudless sky, sunlight flaring
in the fibres; and I remember
the way your lips parted so softly,
and your eyes a distillation of blue
as our kisses took to the air.

Wharfedale

By Bill Appleyard's seat at Loup Scar
among red cornus and beech
we listened to the river applaud the star-

lings for their firework show-
er above yellow larch
and the hill's unfurrowed brow.

Moonshine

A magnificent winter half-moon
      scarred and golden
           sits at my shoulder
all the way up the motorway through Yorkshire.

Rising from the dark horizon it starts out
      the precise colour
           of your hair in summer,
slowly cooling to silver in the closing sky.

I call as soon as I arrive
      thinking only to hear your voice,
           and down the line I find
I'm listening to the moon glinting in your hair.

Two Step

Your footfall on the roof tiles is no more
than the skittering of starlings, jackdaws
pecking at lichen. What are you doing up there
among pincushions of moss, in the night air?
I reach for you wanting to lift you up
cradle you as you let the hammer drop,
moonlight shimmering where the clout nails scatter.
Your fingers slip into my letter-box grip
and words pass between us, but it hardly matters.
We move closer dancing an antique two-step
palm to damp palm; excuses gather
on my lips even before my feet trip
on your hem. Smiling, you open wide
your angel wings, sweep me up in a wash of Chagall red.

aquarel 6 Kandinsky

See! Where life line and
heart line converge, the precise
colour of our love.

In Lucca

In habits as white as death sheets
two squat nuns scuttle across the grass,
disappear into the fortress walls;
there they are again on the ramparts
ahead of me, just where you emerge.
A pair of sparrows flit through
the lopped deodora with its green cones;
they too seem to shadow us.
We dismount at the duomo
where candles flicker in the nave,
wax melts into strange figures around us
and this dark-skinned Jesus is stilled
by his unending burden. As we set off
I watch a wave of dust and leaves
coil around your shoulders.
Even the wind, it seems, wants to cradle you.

The Sadness of Roses

As I drop down from the rise
on a warm summer afternoon
doing eighty on the A34,
Beacon Hill comes into view
like a green female nude.

She is lying on her side, legs drawn up
to hold the shadow
folded between belly and thigh,
her buttocks curving
into the yellow quilt of the field beyond.

Sunlight strobes between slatted trees
as the road levels out. I ease up.
And wonder if you too are contemplating,
at this same moment, the sadness of roses;
how sweet their perfume, how brief their perfection.

Earthed

We carry the fight to one another
all day long
through the combed vineyards,
our hearts parched
and withering like the sunflower crop.

You need to be earthed in the storm
so we make love on the stone floor
and your back
is imprinted with a map
neither of us knows how to interpret.

Soundless

I brought home wild marjoram,
scabious and a pink parsley
to catch your eye in the little kitchen,
leaving my hurt pride by the roadside.
After all our talk I'd wanted to bring
butterflies to stir the air in the bedroom:
flitting blues, graylings, gatekeepers
with watchful eyes, and a jersey tiger
moth, its scarlet flash so startling.
But my hands were too slow in the heat
of the afternoon and, besides, in time
one of us would break the silence,
though the butterflies – soundless
and unexpected – go on
slipping through our fingers forever.

Stars

You are already in bed,
head lying heavy on the pillow,
jaw sagging like medals
on a veteran's chest.

I mooch about downstairs
wondering what tomorrow
may bring for us and why
the moon is not quite round.

I close the French windows
and two soft white stars
fall at my feet – five-pointed,
smelling of jasmine.

Sixty to Ninety Percent
(of Communication is non-Verbal)

It's not just talking – it's not even talking,
it's what your eyes say or your hand
on my shoulder as you bend to kiss me;
it's the way you point to your empty glass,
it's me scribbling through the air when I ask
for the bill, anxious to move on.

It's not just talking – it's what I know
before I enter the room, it's what you knew
before you married me, and did so
nonetheless, it's what I write down
and what I don't, it's what we see together
from the balcony – the way the birds move
and which ones; it's the quarters of the moon
and direction of the wind stirring your hair.

It's not just talking, it's something
that happens whether we're together or apart –
and more so as we grow older – the silence
on the phone, anger or forgiveness, hurt
and tenderness.
                    It's not just flowers
but the colour of the tulips and the choice
of vase (which you are bringing to me now)
and where it's placed, and watching you
and knowing your love – and not just talking.

At the Esterhazy Palace

In the slight hiatus while the interpreter
summons the right word, I am gazing past the speaker
through rococo windows at what was once
a parterre in the ornamental park below,
when a swallow loops the loop over the balustrade
and turns its rose-flushed belly towards me.
In that freeze-frame I see you, head lowered
to a half-open bloom, breathing the scent
of Albertine, or Compassion come early.

Dream Home

That Marc Chagall
has been in the kitchen again
mushing up the summer fruit;

the ceiling's stained purple
and the room is perfumed
with cinnamon and cloves.

You are floating above the sink,
your hand outstretched to me.
Are those wings I see?

Or the bows of your apron strings?
There is myrtle in a vase,
swaying to the sound of Debussy's piano

wafting through the open window;
I feel the bud of my heart opening.
And look! Here's Apollinaire,

poems leaping from his mouth
like tiny birds or showers of sparks;
a loose limbed man is dancing

with the lampstand,
his white quiff a feather
floating out of nowhere.

The Romance of Digging

The breaking of hard ground is good
(I conjectured) the fork probing the clag,
rake and hoe making the tilth;

weighing a clod in the hands,
reckoning by warmth or moisture
how rich the life I held.

The act of digging satisfies
(I thought) the sound of the spade slicing
a spit's depth through good soil,

the sweet symmetry in the grasp,
pivot levering the heavy
earth from here to there.

There is a time to entertain
the old romance of digging (you said)
there is a time to toil.

Back curved like a billhook I was
frozen to the garden fork.
It seemed like a decade.

Consolation

What mattered was not being alone.
And being at one – that, too, mattered:
we were like the river and the river bed.

From the start, and without asking,
your knees were snug against
the small meander of my own,

our fingers were entwined, bone
for bone, at the oxbow of my hip,
your hair giving shade to my tears.

We have lain this way all these years,
sun and moon in the same sky,
rising and setting as one.

Four

Martha's Vineyard, August 1999

The night tide
>has prettified the beach
>>with swags of olive weed

sequinned
>with simple shells:
>>an elegant New England couture

spilling from rock
>to gleaming rock like
>>the contents of someone's

wrecked suitcase, washed ashore.

Papers

The estuary is dotted with divers and waders,
acres of sand stretch to the sea, foxed
and smudged like old papers,
an archive of the endless ebb and flow.
Sheep browse the banks of saltmarsh,
teeter on bent-stick legs above meandering runnels
and, as the train slows, soft white down
floats past the window, travels with us a while
in the slipstream. It'll be two hours
before we get to Manchester
for the flight to Belfast. Meanwhile a grey
cumulus of concrete dust billows
through the streets of Manhattan, sheets
of paper wafting in the updraught.

A Last Swallow

Beneath a fat crumb of half-moon
the breakers pound the sea wall
again and again, their eerie rhythm rumbling
like a thunder-sheet mile after mile
around the darkened bay, from the harbour
all the way out to the Mumbles.

I peer into the sky
hearing the bombers over Kabul.

In the clear blue morning the waves have softened,
footprints and tide-ripples mottle the sand
with its fringe of limp black wrack.
A last swallow swoops and disappears.
In town the first yellow leaves
starburst across the tarmac.

In Kandahar the daylight bombing has begun.

The Inkpot

You have to cross a brook,
climb through a wire fence
under the canopy of pine copse
in the field's hollow angle.

Here watery bubble-pocked bottles
surface from the mat of needles;
blue-green jars, glazed pots,
a spiralled perfume flask, broken-necked,
stuffed with sweet-smelling peat.

Here is a country archive in raised lettering;
"Granny's Delicious Sauce",
"Horse Sheep and Cattle Oil". "Poison".

Kneeling, you feel your wax jacket
stiffen in the cold,
a marble clinks mournfully
in the throat of a pop bottle.

And here a squat octagonal inkpot –
black-caked nib still trapped inside –
that once contained the cleric's mark,
the farmer's contract, a lover's eager words.

Next to it a tiny phial, unstoppered,
green as envy.

Illumination

In the Green Guide
       for Quercy-Périgord
the church at Besse has two stars:
       "mérite un détour".

Its worshipers once hauled
ladders of sweet chestnut
       into the stronghold,
sealed the shutters;
angels still guard the silent doorway.

From floor to ceiling in the chancel
and the apse
frescoes of saints – maps of faith,
       half effaced –
moulder like bloodstains
or the soft tarnish of summer pollen,

their only witnesses the narrow rays
of sunlight that slope
       around the walls
and, like us, vanish.

Norn Iron
for Kevin

The squall carries to me in your voice
like the day we drove up to Glenarm,
rain lashing the cliffs
while breakers yawed
and thrashed against the sea wall.

At times that accent is a moist
breeze working its charm
on the mist over Divis,
or a glimpse of snow in spring
teasing out colours of myrtle and ling.

Dry as coke in Carrickfergus
gasworks, your consonants kick up dust,
crack heads on the kerbs of
Craigavon; your vowels are like rust
on fenceposts and streetlamps,
the snap of tattered flags and emblems.

On Strangford Lough a shag in silhouette,
watchful, as the tide begins to run;
and your voice the echo of its
green lustre and its cockeyed crest.

The Van Morrison Trail

If I had the money I'd buy his voice.
That's what I was thinking as we pulled into Killyleagh
on our way back to Belfast. I thought:
I'd buy that voice, do it up and live in it
down at Coney Island; that stuttering tongue
like a spitting hearth or the creak of floorboards;
in the night the low notes and growls,
wind in the eaves, the whistle of valves
and the small quick feet of the household.

I'd throw out the blinds, use his eyes as windows;
no kitsch trinkets or icons on the sill,
just the riffle of conifers on the skyline,
and moonlight on the mirror of the bay.

Rounding the point I'd be breathing easy,
listening to a breeze scuffing the sand
as autumn turned its back on County Down.

The Crossing
for Christopher

He stands leaning into the wind
as if poised for take-off.
Something surges in his chest
as he stares into the weir's mesmeric grin.
Left foot extending first he steps out
along the wire, its steel hawsers
threaded between stanchions
trimmed with flags, now bright,
now faded. He is Blondin,
epic and absurd above Niagara's mist,
balance-pole flexing like the wings
of a spindly giant bird in slo-mo,
muscles adjusting minutely as each
breath sighs him into weightless flight.

Hepworth's Dream

It feels like falling.

From Leeds city centre
to the garden at St Ives I tumble
through the giddy heart of a tree.

Dark gaurea wood, scented eucalyptus.

The bole opens before me, a swirl
of polished grain, a nut brown arc.
Inside, a mute Atlantic of tendons and veins.

There's more to this once-immense trunk
than you or I can know – its dense matter,
silken surface – so that, looking down
I might be gazing through its branches
at the sky or the ghost-print of a retina.

I stoop.

Through a whirling knot-hole I see
the world outside configured like a giant bell
that swings from side to far side
with the endless rhythm of the toll.
The image of our lives shrinks and swells
in its gleaming brass: the way we part, embrace
and part again.

I'm falling through the tree –
will its cupped hands save me?

Configuration by Barbara Hepworth, Leeds City Art Gallery, January 2003

Strange Attractor

I listen to your voice on the radio
and picture you comfortable
in your little tower of learning,
a pot of cyclamen in the window.
"Poem", you say, and the word falls
from your mouth into deep snow.
I see your thatch of white hair
and the whiskers in which your voice
and his imagination cohabit,
from which the words seem to take flight,
gather, turn without touching,
swoop with perfect gentleness,
their pattern governed by the strange attractor –
a nudged pendulum returning
unfailingly to order. "Drunkenness",
you say, and "roses", the sounds assemble
on your breath in soft layers
like petals folding in the evening air.

On hearing Michael Longley read *Snow* by Louis MacNeice

Treasured Berries
for Keiren

The way she said it, the way she said:
"He bought me champagne – and wild strawberries!"
she might have been that Dashwood girl in thrall
to her imagined Mr Willoughby.

They're *Fragaria Vesca*, she recalled,
fragrant and tiny fruit of the hedgerow.
Fraises des bois, he might have whispered,
it's a Bergman film, a Wedgwood

pattern; courtly and curative,
it's food for the Grizzled Skipper,
love potion, eyebright, scarlet gem
carved to perfection on altar and pillar.

She savoured again the sparkle and sweetness,
the generous gift of a generous giver.

Revelation

In the grass and hedgerows
tiny webs made visible
by September mist.

In the sky Mars, we're told,
invisible to the naked eye,
a red blood cell taken on trust.

With age the skin becomes translucent
making visible the veins
of bodies in motion and at rest.

Passing
i.m. DB

The sun comes up on winter,
bleary-eyed, still sleeping in her make-up.

I'm watching a morning frost slide
from the lawn like a silk sheet from a warm bed.

And I see you, too, slipping from shadow to light;
I feel the warmth of your smile

making the garden draw breath,
the sky flex its soft white limbs,

and the wind-chimes stir, murmuring
something about spring...spring...spring.

The Walk to the Sea

This little gate might have been built of driftwood,
weathered pine curved like axe handles or
the windswept stems of gorse rising from stone walls.

Everything is rounded off, softened with lichen.
It's quiet here, not still – the breeze sees to that
as it scuffs the water, sways leaves, flexes grasses.

The stonechat chitters as it loops along the hedgerow
among hart's tongue and baler twine. Above the field
a crow circles, slopes back to its gatepost.

A heron hunches on a mound, turns his back
to me as I round the inlet. The arc of the bay
glows pink and the sea rolls back on shingle

casting up the skeleton of a drowned boat
whose salt-washed ribs remind me
of a gate built of driftwood.